Within Walking Distance

WITHIN
WALKING
DISTANCE

Poems by
ELLIE ALTMAN

Illustrations by
Emily Kalwaitis

Copyright © 2023 Ellie Altman
Illustrations by Emily Kalwaitis

ellie@elliealtmanpoet.com
www.elliealtmanpoet.com

ISBN 979-8-218-04313-1

Edited and designed by Tell Tell Poetry

Printed in the United States of America
First Printing, 2023

In memory of Miss Sweet Potato Pie, called Tato (2010-2021). My first Vizsla, she took me out in nature every day beneath the sun, the moon, and the clouds—no matter the weather.

CONTENTS

ACKNOWLEDGMENTS

Within Walking Distance is the creation of three collaborators: artist Emily Kalwaitis, poet and editor Lindsay Lusby, and myself. I am grateful for this partnership of equals.

I also wish to thank the wonderful team at Tell Tell Poetry, especially Kallie and Maxine, who helped me to realize my vision for this chapbook of poems and art, bringing my manuscript to life as a beautiful printed book.

Finally, thank you to my adopted home—the town of Chestertown on Maryland's Eastern Shore—where everything I need is within walking distance.

WITHIN WALKING DISTANCE

THE PANDEMIC'S SHIMMERING LINING

Poetry calls us to pause. There is so much we overlook,
while the abundance around us continues to shimmer,
on its own.
—Naomi Shihab Nye

What if
      this is a snowy night and
           we are crossing a bridge,
                  opening a window, or
      stepping beyond a threshold
           to discover a bright dusting and
                all is changed,
     living together with
        less of more and
            more of less.
Stores and schools are closing.
We are hunkering down
     under quilts
           stitched with swatches of our children's
               baptismal and wedding dresses,
     staying off the streets and
        in our solitude
            awaiting a dawn
                to awaken us
to paths mysteriously carved
     overnight through the snow
        that will take us
           wherever we need to go.

SAFE PASSAGE

A narrow passage between Sam's Coffee Shop
and the town's only jewelry store—
the foraging grounds for a witch's apothecary, I imagine
she crouches there beneath
her dark deep-pocketed garb
gathering for her cauldron.

An eerie place,
hiding something,
tree roots spread
large tendrils along the surface
of the cramped path
threatening to trick and
deny a steady footing.

An ever so faint whiff of weed
mixes with nature's detritus and
clings to the brick walls holding
the night sky in a narrow chute.
As we walk single file,
the fallen leaves crispy-crunch mixes
with the thin quicksand layer
of gravel and grit,
percussive sounds reverberate
in all directions.

A rimless Tupperware bowl
set out against the foundation lattice,
marks a gateway for small feral creatures,
brown gruel mush dried
into the corners of the stained container,
its fishy smell dissipates into the frigid air,
its lid lost long ago makes it

an ideal cat bowl, and where
my dog seeks after-dinner treats.

She, always hopeful, remains
oblivious to the strangeness of this place.
We travel most nights together
through this convenient shortcut
from Cross Street to the town parking lot.
I never dare look back.

LEFT IDLING

At the dog park on Monday,
from an idling mower
a town grounds crewman
calls for my attention,
Is that your car?
Move it.
My car is parked on the asphalt pad at the sign:
NO VEHICLES BEYOND THIS POINT.
He directs me to park
on the grass
where there is no sign
indicating parking is permitted.

Only days later,
my second offense,
now in the Acme grocery store parking lot.
I return to my car after a quick stop,
load four bags inside the rear hatch,
a town police officer approaches,
It is against the law to leave a car idling.

My coddled pooch rests in 68 degrees
of the car's AC
listening to NPR.
The officer suggests,
Leave your dog at home.

Later, I Google laws prohibiting
car idling and learn
to warm a vehicle on a winter morning
warrants a hefty fine
as a mandate for the environment.
No one spoke for the needs
of dogs left idling
in summertime.

THREE SHADBUSHES

She lined the entrance walk with three shadbushes a year after she moved in. They replaced three fat yews that died suddenly her first summer in the house. Their needles browned as if she had put a torch to them. She pled not guilty, yet there was cause to doubt. On daily trips down the front walk to collect her newspaper before breakfast and again at noon for the mail, she would cast her eyes toward the lifeless yews, as if they were part of her collection of heirloom stitchery, crewelwork, cross-stitch, and crochet. When she swept the walk, dust and leaves clouded the air around her, stymieing her vision to replace the yews. Week after week, what did passersby think of the owner of the welcome-yellow house with dead shrubs—a gaping hole in its otherwise cheerful smile? The talk surely escalated.

She is not tending her garden.
She is a bit odd.
She is a bad mother.
She is a bad citizen.
She is evil.

And then two burly landscapers arrived in a tall-sided truck with a protective fabric draping three balled and burlapped shadbushes, a dolly, shovels, and mulch. They made haste to dig out the dead yews, and as landscape dancers turned a sweaty job of hoisting, balancing, and lifting into a performance graced with balletic moves and reaches. Bringing each shadbush by dolly to its planting spot, they eased them into the dark friable soil carefully burying each at just the right depth, artfully turning them in place like lifting the prima ballerina for an audience to see her delicate limbs, fingers, and pruned layers of floating crinoline perfection. She admired how quickly the men worked, without sparing any care.

They swept away the evidence and packed their tools having magically turned toll into dance. And now, at day's end, slipped away behind the curtain to repair and repeat their performance

> tomorrow and the next day,
> over and over,
> day after day,
> week after week.

Her three shadbushes thrive.

"WHAT DO YOU DO?"

he asks.
Our paths cross frequently
in the evenings
at the dog park,
but I don't know his name.
I know he is Virginia's former husband,
and he walks her manic Brittany spaniel, Lacy,
because he adores her—
Lacy, not Virginia.
Though I suspect
he adores Virginia too.

Almost 40 years ago,
as a recent college graduate,
I would have dismissed this question
as intrusive, a lack of social gravitas.
My evenings at the park are
to let my dog, Sweet Potato, off-leash
to run in the treeless lawn and, for me,
to walk its perimeter, around and around—
my daily constitutional—
while I listen with my earbuds
to podcasts about righting wrongful convictions.

Collared, I will answer his question.
A flippant response
comes first to mind,
Just what I want to do.
But I compose myself and my words.

There is no need to become agitated
about his sincere curiosity, even if
it is none of his beeswax.
I forego my adolescent angst
to tell the truth:
I am a poet.
I do what I do.

GARDEN CHORES

No reason not
to make this a perfect day:

> a forecast of cloudless sun
> and warm fall temperatures
> well into the 50s.

What's to keep me from
those garden chores
   I see every day
      and say:

> *if it weren't*
>
> > *so cold*
> > *so windy*
> > *so wet.*

And then a perfect day arrives
   and I find myself lying in bed

> reading the final chapter of
> this month's book club book,

when every day

> the clothes crammed into my closet
> need to be sorted for the season

and every day I say:

> *give this stuff away or*
> *move it to the attic.*

Who is taking a bet
to see how I spend this warm buttered-toast autumn day?

Who guesses that I clean out the freezer instead?
Or finish sewing a costume
for the weekend's Victorian house tour?

There are so many ways to feel productive:

housekeeping

meal planning

dog-walking

poetry writing, and

bill paying.

Again, I check the forecast,
now promising three more days of sun.

I choose to do my garden chores

tomorrow
or maybe the next day.

THE CURTAIN RISES
ON THE RIOT OF LIFE

He rarely speaks at dinner—
eats quickly,
helping himself
to seconds.
He is pleased
with his meal.
She sits across from him
rarely taking
seconds.
She raises her head
to look beyond—
through the patio doors
to her garden,
the curtain rises
on a three-ring circus
of acrobats, dancers, and fireworks
in celebration of her toil,
in a riot of magenta,
lemon, lavender, and ruby
exploding in the treetops' reaches
and the understory,
edging the stone path
with shooting-star goldenrod,
twirling-dervish salvia,
velvet-silver lamb's ear,
spinning-spray fuchsia.
This riot of life is set against
the stage's backdrop of manicured privet.
The entire cast rallies
with Olympian determination,
surpassing all that have come before,

defying the critics.
The dancers in full regalia
fill the stage
before taking their late summer bow
as the musicians—
the birds and bees, the frogs and crickets—
rise from their seats
applauding the season's last show.
The earth's creepy crawlers
take witness
from their amphitheater
in the litter of rotting twigs and leaves.

She smiles, satiated
by the evening's pyrotechnics.
Her eyes soften.
She drops her head
to the foreground and
her husband's unruly white hair
and unshaven face.

STREET SMORGASBORD

Our town streets are a veritable delicatessen
for my dog. Today her nose led her to two delicacies,
a piece of pizza—the main course—and a Pop-Tart for dessert.

The pizza found along Mill Street in the pachysandra on the east side
of the old high school building, now the county offices.
The Pop-Tart in plain sight at the base of the electrical pole
at the corner of Maple and Queen Streets.

Over the years, she has retrieved
a Slim Jim, still in its wrapper, hanging from
a Nellie Stevens holly branch next to Houck's Men's Shop,
half of a roast beef sandwich at the curb across from Sam's Coffee Shop,
and smashed or partially eaten croissants, muffins, and cookies
scavenged any direction within a block of Evergrain Bakery.

What she is sure to find each day are chicken bones.
Most often they are small weathered bones stripped of meat and gristle.
But on a good day, a pile of wings in the middle of the street
where Queen and High intersect,
and reliably in our neighborhood's new 7-Eleven parking lot.

And also in front of our town's most desirable historic properties on Water Street,
routinely on the sidewalks and in the shrubbery
where crews are restoring and repairing nineteenth-century homes.
On any route, her dog walks are a stroll down an all-you-can-eat cafeteria line.

What's your secret, I ask,
to your svelte physique when you serve yourself
from every swale, seep, and sweep?

Tack, she whispers, nose to the ground.
Tack, I observe,
the incessant practice of seemingly
nonsensical zigzag maneuvers.

Never head into the wind, she continues,
dart and dash,
tweak and refine,
lust for wander.

BEAUTY CONTEST AT THE DOG PARK

I do feel terrible about it—
my irritation with the wife
joined by her husband
walking the perimeter of
our town's manicured dog park
as their mixed-breed pup
darts to and from them.

I puzzle why one of these two,
husband or wife,
wastes time doing what the other
could do alone.
I learn the husband would rather
be figuring out why Netflix
on his computer
flashes, "Not Available."

Yet, mostly, my irritation settles on
the wife's tedious telling of her love affair
with their precious dog, Promise—
her insipid claims about the dog's long whiskers
cute like a seal's and
a rear end of soft white fur
like a German Shepherd's.

With unabashed disdain,
I dismiss the wife's drivel.
It goes without saying:
my sleek mahogany Vizsla,
Hungarian aristocracy-bred
to flush fowl
from fields and swamps,
is the dog park's reigning beauty.

OVER COFFEE

The buzz of a blizzard forecast permeates the town—
fleece-lined jackets hang haphazardly on ladder-back chairs.
Customers sit deep in their seats
with this gift of uncommitted time,
an unexpected refund,
a debt now paid.
Worries evaporate into thin air.

We enter the bakery's narrow doors,
a brief lull between the early-morning-coffee and the lunch-sandwich crowds,
claiming a table in the middle where the floorboards don't match,
sliding our chairs close, knees touching.
We begin our visit with talk about our good fortune—
living in our town
all within walking distance.
Storefront windows display
rough-hewn linen tunics, crunchy fair-trade decor,
local artisan wares, used books, wine, and cheeses.
The prime street-corner retail space
where the county historical society
rotates exhibits of memorabilia
from attics and sheds.

After long, daunting years
bearing witness to her husband's decline—
he now honored and buried,
she in a new car
with travel plans for the fall,
stepping into a new dawn.
As I begin my journey
with a failing husband,
she makes her generous offer—
Call anytime.

GLOBAL WARMING

Just to read the word *bemuse* amuses—
irresistibly sweet, coy, and flirtatious,
juxtapose the nonsensical and consequential,
caught in a tangle of delight,
yet maybe promising the opposite
or something in between.

Oh, to live an entire life in this soft spot
taking nothing too seriously,
never breaking a sweat
nor stranded painfully
beneath the albatross of ominous clouds.

Like this morning's brief exchange with the carpenter
balanced atop the neighbor's pergola
doing repairs in the middle of February
as if it were spring,
the damage done in a terrifying night storm
when winds shrieked and wrestled
muscular bare limbs from
the neighborhood's largest oaks
and sycamores to the ground
into impenetrable piles.

Disregarding the calendar's claim that winter is here,
temperatures tease spring's early arrival.
The carpenter greets me with unseasonable cheer.
I respond, bemused,
If this is global warming, bring it on.

LIFE'S FORECAST

She dreams of town life
tuned to a Tibetan singing bowl,
and at the top of each hour,
the bell tower bathes residents
in high vibrations.
Tree-lined streets tame traffic,
and trash collection is timely.
Where tastings, toastings, and togetherness
routinely fill the town square.

Today's Sunday paper,
tossed onto her front stoop before sunrise,
folded neatly to reveal page one's
top-of-the-fold news.
The headline reads:
IF THIS IS WINTER, WE'LL TAKE IT.
A slight cast of reasonable doubt in the subtitle:
January's warmth may spell trouble for some plants, though.

Below *The Sunday Star* banner,
a large color photograph carries a caption
for the day's biggest news:
Warm weather brings out fishing enthusiasts.
A robust gentleman is pictured on a new dock,
well-appointed with copper-topped pilings.
He sits deep in an orange, canvas umbrella chair
with a straw hat and pipe and, at his feet,
a small neat tackle box and a homemade sandwich
and three chocolate-dipped sugar cookies
packed in a recyclable tote.

This is her town life
with its fast-breaking news
tossed at her feet
announcing it is time to go fishing.

ABOUT THE AUTHOR

Ellie Altman's poems have been published in *Gyroscope Review*, *The Shore*, and *The Broad River Review*. A finalist for ESWA's 2021 Crossroads Writing Contest, she has attended workshops taught by Jeff Coomer, Barbara Crooker, Ishion Hutchinson, Kelly Grace Thomas, and Sue Ellen Thompson, among others. Altman began writing poetry in 2014, after retiring as director of Adkins Arboretum. She lives on Maryland's Eastern Shore with her husband and her beloved Viszla pup. *Within Walking Distance* is her first chapbook.

Lightning Source UK Ltd.
Milton Keynes UK
UKHW050620080223
416654UK00004B/277